Churches

Also by Kevin Prufer

Strange Wood
The Finger Bone
Fallen from a Chariot
National Anthem
In a Beautiful Country

Churches

Kevin Prufer

Four Way Books
Tribeca

Please direct all inquiries to:
Editorial Office
Four Way Books
POB 535, Village Station
New York, NY 10014
www.fourwaybooks.com

Library of Congress Cataloging-in-Publication Data

Prufer, Kevin.
[Poems. Selections]
Churches / Kevin Prufer.
pages cm
Selected poems previously published in various periodicals and journals.
ISBN 978-1-935536-43-7 (alk. paper)
I. Title.
PS3566.R814A6 2014
811'.54--dc23
                              2013036094

This book is manufactured in the United States of America and printed on acid-free paper.

Four Way Books is a not-for-profit literary press. We are grateful for the assistance
we receive from individual donors, public arts agencies, and private foundations.

This publication is made possible with public funds from the National Endowment for the Arts.

and from the New York State Council on the Arts, a state agency.

[clmp]

We are a proud member
of the Council of Literary Magazines and Presses.

Distributed by University Press of New England
One Court Street, Lebanon, NH 03766

CONTENTS

One

Two

ONE

Potential Energy Is Stored Energy

When the bomb tore through the train,
it cut the first-class cabin into halves.
Inside, the wealthy travelers mostly died,
though here and there
                    one cupped his bleeding ears
or looked around,
              confused. Where the car had split,
snow blew in,
          capping the upturned drink cart,
a lady's coat, the dying porter
                  who smiled
up at the sky.

+

           Such constellations
blown-out windows make,
their million shards sprinkled over snow.
                   Such filigree
where the hot glass sank
             and cooled—

+

For hours,
         the bomb knelt in its suitcase, half-aware
of the thrum of wheels on tracks,
                 the churn and tip
when the train turned
          or, following the river, cut west
along its banks,

+

and the dying porter thought about his son.

+

For hours, its little heart had ticked
                              on its rack
above the ladies' heads. It heard the old men
playing cards,
                    the rattling drink cart.
It dreamed about a plume of smoke,
the second when the casement cracks
and up to the Lord with the splinters
                              and the glass—

+

Snow fell on his face and melted there,
snow in his hair,
                    covering his lapel—and his only son,
how he felt his heart beat through him
when he cradled him
                    or helped his wife
to bathe him in the sink,
                    the heat coiled in the infant's body—
it was years ago.

+

Dear Lord, dear Lord,
                    the bomb kept saying,
curled in its suitcase like a prayer,
                         muffled on its rack—

+

And the baby in the bath was burning up with fever,
so they soaked him there, filled the tub with ice
and smoothed his hair. *Oh, beautiful*
                         black-eyed baby,
his wife was singing,
                    while she stroked his cheek
and the doctor never came—

+

                    Dear Lord, I give this to you:
each lady's black felt hat, each full glove.
                    I give you coats
and shards of frosted glass that decorate the first-class cabin's
perfect ceiling.
          I give you books and cards and windowpanes,
the men who dream behind them—

+

                    And the heat inside the baby—
he recalled it now as down the thick snow fell
and covered up his eyes—
                    he was ungodly hot, a burn

no ice could draw.
                    He won't last long like this,
his wife was crying,
                    but still they bathed him—

+

and when the heat tore through it,
                                        the ceiling split
and crashed into the floor. The derailed train
tipped and buckled,
                    curled and died. And in its final moments,
the doomed bomb smiled—

+

I give this to you, Lord,
                    in a wisp of smoke, in splinters
scattered in the wind and love.

+

The porter
            slept where the train had wrenched apart.
His son,
            pinch-faced, stayed in the sink, grew hotter still,
and could not breathe.
                    Oh breathe, breathe, his wife was saying,
while the great unmelting snows concealed his eyes,
and up to the waiting heavens
                    this black plume rose.

LOVE POEM

They'd installed ten cannons on the moon.
        All night long
I watched the tracers fall.
      They lit the dim world up
so I could see
     the Tetons' row of jagged teeth,
the Great Lakes winking
       like mirror shards
or fields of Kansas wheat,
       lustrous in the magnesium glare.

+

I hovered in the thinning air,
       my half-illuminated
observation pod
     atilt along an orbit's line
while far below the forests burned,
        their black smoke thickening
the troposphere.
    And where

+

were you? Oh, far away,
      aboard another pod
while the cannons fired and fired,
       and the moon grew
strange and speckled over
      in the airless gloom
of ammunition and its backward kick—

                                        while the moon
wobbled from the force of it—

+

                          hovering
above a distant land,
                    your craft grown sick
so the engine smoked and died.
                              Coasting to the ground
in the pulsing air
                    then hiding in a cave
to keep the heat
                    and burn away. I imagined it grew
far too warm in there.

+

I hadn't much more fuel,
                          so passed above our house
and watched it through the scope.
                              It smoked and shook
and then the porch roof caved.
                          The windows all blew out—
they looked like puffs of glitter
                    from my height.

+

                                    Still,
I thought I'd set my weak pod there
                          and walk among
our swiftly burning trees,
                    the unripe fruit
that sizzled on the ground.
                          It was a lovely moon
we used to sit below,
                    the moon that burned the city down
and set the fields aglow,
                    moon that glittered hotly
while its great guns fired.
                    It was an angry moon
that made me miss you so.

From Inside the Avalanche

Three months I've hung here like a yolk
and they might not find me
                        until the snow melts.
My bent arm could tumble up a skier,
or my cracked legs slip
               and pull me farther
down the slope.

+

But for now I have made myself a dome
                      to curl inside.
I have made a cold, cold womb.
                And when the sun
comes out, it fills me with a pale blue glow
I can see my frost-bit fingers by.
                In this filtered light,
my brain is a nimbler thing, and strange. It loves
the slow derangements distance brings.
                Nights I cannot tell
which way is up.

+

Such wine I drank to bring me
to a place like this. And then I sobered up.
                Such pills I took,
and down to the depths with them.
               And films and books
to snuff my dull mind out—

                    I turned the music up
until my eardrums flapped,
               and always
I came back, back, back—

+

Above, I hear the whoosh
and swerve of skis, the thump of children and the creak
of gears.
        Once or twice I poked my fingers through
and felt the cool winds rumble down the slope.

+

I suppose I should dig myself out.
                  I suppose
I might shamble down the hill
and find the ski lodge where a great fire burns.
(And how they all would gawk
              at my return!
And how they'd shout!)
          Ice-encrusted,
black where my thin skin froze, where my wrist-bones
snapped and my nose fell off,
            I'd pool and steam
among the skiers
        and find a bit of comfort in their warmth.

POETRY

That car was burning. Are there any questions? It rested on its roof, flipped. Are there any questions? The windshield had scattered its pointed little thoughts over the pavement. Hello?

The wheels were muscle only and knew little, spinning pointlessly against the air. The radio glowed like my heart, and it sang like my heart.

Even now, the man inside tries not to sleep. Anyone?

How darkness makes beautiful the same fire daylight ignores. How that queer flower blooms best at night.

I saw the whole thing. Here I am. Up here.

It's a rickety balcony I'm standing on. Then the car crash turned the houselights on, so there you all are

gathered at your windows. The ambulance purred to a stop, its great red heart flashing over the houses.

It warms the skin, and when I move, the planks below me want to break—

Won't you cut his seatbelt with those clippers? Won't you haul him out so I can see?

—then down I'll fall past my neighbors' windows, down I'll tumble to where that car is burning, to where that man sleeps inside it and the column of smoke is invisible in the night

and you won't notice my descent, no, you won't cry out, you won't turn and gather around me, you won't ask me any questions at all.

Paper Cup

In those days, you could leave your child at the city's edge for the wolves.

You could wrap your child in leaves or in rags; you could put it in a basket and set it afloat

or sew it in a deerskin and drop it from a cliff.

You could smear it with soot or with dirt and give it to gypsies or dogs,

or, to guarantee a stormless sea, strap it to the bow of one of many ships.

+

Here are your pills.

Thalidomide and hydrocodone and Diamox: three little bugs in a paper cup.

It rained all day, and then it snowed and you said, *Look at the Lortab,*

and down it came, burying the cars in the parking lot, sifting through the trees, pilling up the windowsills

until the antiseptic city grew stunned and senseless

and you laughed and *Here are your pills,* I said four hours later,

Here are your pills, every four hours, while down the Lortab fell.

+

In troubled times, a man might offer up his child for mercy, firewood, venison.

Those parsnips grew best among the fists of buried children.

And how the peeled onion resembled the soft face that gave it life.

The gods loved most that man who offered what he cherished,

and from the gardens came the scent of richly nourished lilacs.

+

You could plant me in the ground until I sprout.

You could put me in a box and tape it closed and set it to the wind-wracked sea.

Pennants tear themselves to pieces in a storm. String me up and I will bring
you luck.

Or put me in a paper cup and swallow me.

+

While you slept, I fingered the rootlings and felt the rhizomatic soil bear down.

Here I am, among the tubers. Here I am, in a bottle of pills.

+

Percocet to make the crying stop. Triazolam for sleep,

so down the Lortab fell to make your breathing calm, down it fell upon the houses

of your youth, down upon familiar snow-lit streets, the yellow rooms you raised me in,

where *Here I am*, I told you, *Here I am, look at me*, calling from the playroom,

Here are your pills, as I held them to you in a paper cup.

+

From the high flagpole or a treetop, a child's cry was a warning

to anything that meant his father harm.

And while you slept, I bobbed on the current so the stars spun above my head.

+

Long ago, you swaddled me in blankets, tied me to a raft, and nudged me from the shore.

And so I drifted through the night, my cries chipping the black water.

Those who heard me smiled and wished you health.

And years later, king of a far country, I came back to comfort you in your infirmity.

+

Wake up.

I'm sorry I've been gone so long.

Now the snow is pooling in the streets. It slips in clots along the rooftop's slope.

Here are the last of your pills, little white zeros in a cup.

El Paso

One of the three salesmen in the Quality Inn lobby closes his phone

then tells the others, *My wife wants to know why the sand around here tastes
    like salt,*

and, having no answer, the other two laugh and turn to the clerk, a plump
    Mexican kid, who shrugs and hands them their keycards,

so they wheel their suitcases into the courtyard, past the empty pool,

and find their rooms, where he calls her back, says, *Maybe it's the ancient
    oceans. I miss you, too.*

Then the sun goes down on Wendy's and Big Lots, and the windshields in
    the used car lot glitter in the sodium lights,

and the thousand bioluminescent jellyfish of Juarez glow in the valley.

+

The kid looks up from his textbook and out the lobby window thinking
    about Cenozoic oceans

while the tax office says, *Habla Espanol,* says, *Drop-In's Welcome!* and
    Open Sunday's,

and the headlights swim past the Ventura Café and Pier One,

and lightning unnerves the Franklin Mountains, strange lightning so
    El Paso shimmers up to the sky and the sky shimmers down on it,

and then it's raining, fat hot drops decorating the lobby windows so the
    street turns kaleidoscopic in the storm.

+

He's got a brother studying for the police and a brother chased down the
    highway and shot through the windshield and buried in Juarez,

and he's got a row of ammonite fossils above his bed, some pyritized
    and glittering, others preserved in sandstone, limestone, half-
    hollowed and broken,

and the rain comes harder now, rushing down Santa Fe St and Mesa St,
    washing the candy wrappers and paper bags into Juarez,

where his brother crystallizes in the cemetery and his other brother
    sleeps through the storm with his wife beside him,

+

and in his room, the salesman looks at the storm, says *Fuck it,* turns up
    his collar and runs through the rain to his car.

And then he's pulling out of the parking lot into the street, and then he's
    entering the traffic's flow.

He heard about the Mexican girls at Mestizo Bar on Schuster Ave

and he's caught in the rainwater, pushing him down the hill, faster and
    faster, into the valley, sweeping him away,

+

while the kid behind the check-in desk thinks about his dead brother
    turning to pyrite,

how he'll be golden in fifty million years, how they'll all be golden,

and below ground, where the rainstorm seeps, the brachiopods are
    sleeping, the trilobites and the ammonites,

and all the other dead, glittering or not, crystallized, desiccated, half-
    rotted in the torrent,

their fingers gone thick and loose, their chests caved in, their eyeholes
    empty,

and, yes, he should have said, *yes the sand tastes like salt, but it is an old salt,
    it is very old,*

and you have to eat a lot of it to love it.

ALLIGATORS

How at the VFW bar, he rolled up his sleeves. Alligators curled around his wrists. *Eighteen of them*, he said. *I just like them, I don't know why.*

How I saw one in the yard and told my ex-wife, *Don't go out there now.*

How an alligator slides backward into its pond the way a ruined man slides into himself.

He fought off six of them with a pool cue. *One of them cut me right here with a goddamn broken bottle.*

An alligator slept on his forearm. One curled around his neck.

How their bellies flatten the grass they move through so you can follow their trails, how they sleep at the pond's edge, hundreds of them along the shore—

Should of known. They come up behind you when you ain't expecting it, hit you on the head with a beer bottle. And for what?

He was halfway drunk, his good eye focused on the row of bottles below the TV set.

I only laughed to keep him quiet.

I'd lost my job a few times recently, my wife was in Connecticut somewhere with my kid, and outside it was nighttime, cicadas lighting up the air with their racket.

You will maybe find arms or legs in its belly.

You will maybe find scratches around its eyes where she tried to fight it off.

You be good now, you hear? You drive safe. You watch your back. You hear?

Sometimes, one comes out at night and crawls along the sidewalks or stalks through the lawn. Sometimes, they're in the swimming pool or your garage, sometimes they're in your living room drinking, they're in your kitchen waving around a broken beer bottle sometimes—

At first I couldn't find my keys. Then I couldn't unlock the door.

In the dark water, the black hearts keep beating.

Where Have You Gone?

In this story,
                while his parents slept below deck,
their young son thought it would be fun
to lower the life raft
                and float beside the ship.

+

But he soon realized he couldn't keep up—the ship
moved much more quickly than he'd thought
                            and his oars
were light and would not catch the waves—

and though he shouted
no one ran to the rails or raised the alarm.

+

And then the ship was far ahead.
Hello, he called
                as it shrank.

+

In their cabin below deck, his parents dressed for dinner.
I don't know, she said.
                You don't know? he said.
I thought he was by the pool. Sorry.
But when he didn't come for dinner,

she grew concerned.
And when the first mate saw the steel prongs
where once the life raft was,
the captain slowed the ship
and radioed the shore.

+

Hello?
he called into the black night.
Hello? he said, softly now,
lying on the raft's wet vinyl. *Hello?*
And the waves lapped the sides,
the raft turning on the current
so the stars spun slowly overhead.

+

In a story she'd read, a boy rose into the sky in a hot air balloon
and was never seen again.
And the stewardess saw him to the gate
but he did not board the plane.
Then the skylight caved beneath his feet
and down he fell into his parents' dinner party
so they stood by the shore
holding a single flipper,
so they looked beneath all the trains
in the rail yard,
so they opened every cabinet in the school,
so they emptied all the boxes in the warehouse.

+

I'm sorry, she told her husband.

　　　　　　　　I thought he was in the pool.

+

The helicopter's beam
　　　　　　　　lit the water's black surface
and confused the waves.
　　　　　　　　Two helicopters and their beams
like long fingers.
　　　　　　　　Three and she could hear their thrum
a mile off.

+

No, no, these were stories about other people.

He was certainly asleep somewhere,
curled in a box
　　　　　　　　where he'd been playing—

+

while in his sleep, the air filled with bees
　　　　　　　　　　　　and he hid
behind the screen door.
　　　　　　　　And then the bees were crawling
over the screen, humming, atop each other,
bees upon bees on the screen
　　　　　　　　he hid behind.

+　　　　　　　　　　25

A refrigerator lay on the junk pile.

                          Inside it, a voice called to her,
said, *Hello?*

          Said, *Would someone please open the door?*
No, no, no,

          his mother told herself. *It's not like that.*
Not a box like that.

+

Their lights were so bright,

                    and they rose and fell

along the horizon.

+

And the bees chewed a hole in the screen
so first one came through,

                  and then another, their thrumming
grown loud and strange,

              and they were on his skin, the boy
whimpering, afraid to swat them away—

+

                      They are so fragile,
she was thinking,

            remembering how, holding him years ago,
it had occurred to her that, like a vase,

                 he, too, might shatter
on the floor.

She weighed him in her arms. It would be so easy,
like a costly vase—

+

        And the sun rising like a hot air balloon,
and in its basket, a child crying for its mother—

+

                            so the waves
glittered strangely in the new day
                while the helicopters
stowed their search lights.

+

And then the bees were very loud,
                roaring over him
while a helicopter hovered above the raft,
                  while it spit
its rope over the sleeping boy—

+

              No, not like that,
she thought, having dropped the vase on the floor,
having dropped the mirror,
            having dropped the hairdryer
and the pills and the scissors and cell phone, *no, not like that,*

while far away they strapped him in
                              and hauled him up—

+

And the empty raft bobbed on the waves—

+

I slept all night long dreaming about bees,
and when I woke up—

+

                    And her husband swept
the shards from the bathroom floor—

+

                              And dreamed about vases—

+

I'm in here, the little voice said.
                    Here I am! I'm in here,
if you'll just unlock the door,
                         if you'll just untie me,
if you'll just turn on the lights,
                    drain the tub,

open the garage door,
                    move aside the rubble—

+

How his face seemed,
                    when she thought of it,
glassy—

+

When days later the life raft washed up on the beach,
other children played inside it
                    pushing it far from shore,
then riding it landwards again.

Churches

In 1981
        in a hotel gift shop outside Phoenix, Arizona,
a little girl stood by the postcard rack, turning it gently.
It creaked.
        She considered a picture of the desert, then
looked around for her mother,
                        who was elsewhere.
She gave the rack a firm push so it spun
gently on its axle,
                smiled, pushed it again,
and the postcard rack wobbled on spindly legs.

And soon she had it spinning
                        so quickly the cards
made long blurry streaks in their rotation, gasps of blue
for sky,
        red for dirt, and then faster,
the girl slapping at it with her hand,
                                grinning at me,
and then a single postcard rose from the rack, spun in the air
and landed at my feet,
                a picture of a yawning canyon,
and then another, handfuls of postcards
rising from the rack,
                turning in the air
while the girl laughed
                        and her oblivious mother, at the other end
of the store, bought a map or a box of fudge,
and then the air was full of pictures
                                all of them shouting

Phoenix, Phoenix, Phoenix,
$$\text{twirling and falling}$$
until the empty postcard rack
groaned once more, tipped,
and crashed through the window.

+

There ought to be a word
$$\text{that suggests}$$
how we're balanced at the very tip of history
and behind us
$$\text{everything speeds irretrievably away.}$$

"It's called *impermanence,*"
$$\text{the little girl said,}$$
looking at the mess of postcards on the floor.
"It's called *transience,*" she said,
$$\text{gently touching the broken window.}$$
"It's called *dying,*" she said.
$$\text{It was 1981}$$
and the clerk ran from behind the counter,
$$\text{stood before us.}$$
The girl smiled sweetly.
The postcard rack glittered
$$\text{in the sun and broken glass.}$$
He turned to me and my face grew hot.
I couldn't help it. I was blushing.

+

In 2009, my father lay in a hospital bed
gesturing sweepingly with his hands.
                              "What are you doing?"
I asked him. "I'm building a church," he said.
"You're making a church?" I said.
                              "Can't you see?" he said.
He seemed to be patting something
in the air, sculpting something—a roof?—that floated above him.
The hospital room was quiet and white.
"What kind of church is it?" "I'm not finished."
"Is it a church you remember?"
                              "Goddammit," he said. "Can't you see I'm busy?"

+

It was 1988 and I stood in line for my diploma
and my father took a picture
                              that I've lost now.
1984 and there we are
                              around a campfire I can't remember.
It was 2002
            and his cells began to divide wrongly, first one
deep in the wrist bone, then another
                              turned hot and strange,
deformed, humpbacked and fissured,
                              queer and off-kilter,

one after the other,
          though no one would know it for years.

+

"It's called *dying*," the girl said,
               while the postcards suspended
in the air like a thousand days.
            I reached out to touch one,
then another,
        and all at once they fell to the floor.

Then the clerk said
          I was paying for the window,
where were my parents,
          and who was going to pay
if I didn't know where my parents were?
             And the girl
smiled from behind the key chains
           and her mother
pursed her lips at the far end of the store.
            The window
had a hole in it through which a dry breeze came.
The postcards shifted on the floor.

+

Years later,
       my father was still making a church

with his hands.

               "They do that," the nurse said,
patting his head like he was a little boy.

                                 He was concentrating
on his church, though,

                    his hands shaping first what seemed to be
the apse, then fluttering gently down the transepts.
He sighed heavily, frustrated,

                   began again.
"Can I bring you anything else?" the nurse asked.
"No," I said. "Thanks."

                  "Are you sure?" She watched him
tile the roof, watched his finger shape another arch.
And then it was much later.

                  He'd fallen asleep.
Outside, snow covered up the cars.

+

"It's called *forgetting*," the girl said,

                   while the clerk
watched me and I blushed. "Until there's nothing left."
And a breeze entered

             through the hole in the window.
"And then you're out of time," she said,

                   and shrugged.
Some of the cards were face up on the floor:

                   two burros
climbing a craggy slope,

          the Grand Canyon like a mouth

carved in the earth, a night-lit tower like a needle.

          I was sweating now,
but I couldn't speak.

     And then I was running from the shop,
past the fountain and the check-in desk,
down the tiled hall to the hotel pool,
where my father lay on a plastic beach chair,

         reading a book about churches.
Sunlight flecked his chest.

      His hair was wet from swimming.
"What's the trouble?" he asked.

+

First
  his cells were thick and soupy,
clotted and aghast.

      Then they were spinning
through the air.

     And it was 1986 and rain
drummed on the roof.

      Or it was snowing, years later,
in Cleveland,
    his hands working the air
while the nurse stood in the doorway and sighed.

         Wind and sun,
a bright day, a lovely day
      to lie by the hotel pool and read
about how men spent lifetimes building them

and never saw them finished.

MATCHSTICKS

Here's another match for you, I told him,
and here's another, and another,
so they kept bouncing off his fine black jacket, his little cap,
so they glittered on the asphalt at his feet.
Don't just stand there pumping gas, I told him, flicking another match.
Who do you think you are?

+

Said the doctor who opened me up: *Will you look at that?* His glove in my
gut, his long, low whistle until *Enough*, I said, *Enough!* But he would not
hear me, his glove tracing the little black polyps along the intestinal wall,
button-like, Braille-like, like nothing he'd ever seen. And *Enough*, I told him,
rising above the table, *Enough*, floating higher still, over his shoulder while,
with that sickle balanced so carefully between his thumb and index finger,
he lengthened the incision.

+

I'd been a soldier in the war, I'd marched through hot winds, I'd slept in
the heat, spent, I'd watched the moon come up drunk as shit, I'd put on the
visor, the 80 lbs of gear, I'd knelt over the device in the hot sun, in the dust,
I'd clipped the tripwires and the device held its breath, it held its breath, it
did not kill me.

+

Nice car, I said, as a lit match bounced across the hood and landed at his feet.
Shithead, I said, letting another match bounce off the gaspumps.

+

. . . and after the haruspex examined the entrails of the strangled goat, he turned to Augustus and shook his head. He need provide no other signal, for the intestines themselves were blackened as if after many days in the sun . . .

+

So the doctor made a note in his pad, so he sawed my breast bone almost through, so he cracked it with his hand, so he weighed my lungs on a scale, so he touched my heart with his gloved hand, so he touched my guts, so I hovered above his head saying *Please stop, please stop—*

+

And *Read* the CO told me. *You got to get out of your own head, read a book, any goddamn book, a comic book, I don't care.* He lent me one about the battle in the Teutoburg Forest and later asked me how I liked it—

+

And the long black car was idling by the gas pump,
and that man leaned against the bumper looking out over the city
where the long arteries along the river glowed with cars,
where the smokestacks bloomed at their tips with blue flame,
where the airplanes came in and in and in like hot breaths and
who the fuck do you think you are? I asked, lighting another match, tossing it
so it arced over the hearse and landed at his feet—

+

And the children laughing in the street while I stood, my face sweat-streaked—they would not see me tremble—and I removed the plastic visor, what good was it?—and the device lay there in the dirt, its entrails glistening in the sun.

+

. . . the goat's intestines simmered on the altar, for no woman would clean them away. And it was a grave disappointment to Augustus, for now he was committed, for now the legions had departed, for now—

. . . in retrospect, it was perhaps not a bad decision,
the legions over the Rubicon and Varus a competent general, a fine
figure, the entrails not so black as they looked, a trick of light—

+

The doctor snapped off his gloves, rinsed his blades, and left the room—so what could I do but hover around the blackened light bulbs and watch myself not breathe?

+

It did not kill me, not that one and not the next one or the one after that. The little wires glittering, spent, dead by the roadside. We'd go on and on and then we'd drink or read, our fingers shaking, our heads thick, our insides gone to rot—

+

I was out of matches.
He collected his receipt and folded it carefully into his wallet.
When he started the car, I slid into the back seat where it was warm,
where I could sleep while we rumbled down the long artery,

while we dipped below the skin and the hearse hummed so soothingly, like
a spinning saw, the doctor saying, *Will you look at that?*

+

When only two soldiers returned to Rome, both gravely wounded, carrying the
head of Varus in a bag—
     . . . his body spoiled among the trees,
     . . . his body fit for crows, blackened and spilled, pecked at—
Give me back my legions, Augustus cried, and this was a lesson for an otherwise
great man who thought to have his way—

+

I was talking when they zipped me closed
and rolled me down the white hallway and out the back door,
my insides stitched up tight, the black car idling:

+

You clip the tripwire, you cut the vein, you pay attention
to the black one, the polyps, what are we doing here? Even now,
I said, floating above the parking lot, hands full of matchsticks,
even now I am useful. Cut my stitches, open me up once more,
look at the coils inside me.

INSIDE THE BODY

He left the clamp inside the body

and only that night, lying in bed, did he realize what he'd done.

This is why he couldn't sleep. This is why the next morning he was so
    tired he left a safety pin inside another body.

This is why he forgot the sponge in the rib cage, the scope in the
    abdomen,

this is why he forgot the tweezers and the asepto bulbs, the surgical
    retractor and the needle.

He had such worries he couldn't rest. And all day long, he bent over
    sleeping bodies holding scalpels

that inevitably he'd leave inside them before he sewed them up.

+

When I woke, it was to a bright light and a god was bending over me.

He's coming to, God said, and his face grew large and blotted out the glare.

Dear God, I was thinking, *I cannot feel my legs. Dear God, I am like a mind
    floating over a table on which my body is sleeping.*

+

The university professor was saying that the body exists to demarcate the
    liminal space between the living and the dead;

the body, she was saying, is a contested zone between presence and absence,
between consciousness and eternal sleep, between the earth and the
afterlife, between ourselves and the terrifying ambiguity of the void.

The students wrote all of this down.

The body, she said, is a foreign object, neither the person we know nor the
empty husk that person leaves behind. It is a symbol unmoored
from the limitations of meaning.

+

My body was full of foreign objects: bonesaw, syringe, several yards of gauze.

I could see them glittering as I rose above the surgical lamps.

+

At night, the surgeon dreamed of the objects he'd lost inside his patients

lined up on long windowsills, glittering in the playful sunshine—

steel retractors, suction tips, drills and calipers.

In his dreams, his surgical mask fell off his face into the body. His glasses, too.

In his dreams, he rolled up a white paper hospital gown, stuffed it into the
incision and sewed the patient up.

His wife was leaving him. He'd had too much to drink. *Are you all right?*
the nurses asked, shaking their heads. *Are you sure?*

+

We bury the body or we leave it on a ledge to the darkness, we tie rocks
around its legs and sink it in the sea, we put it in a bag and throw
it from a cliff, we remove the indifferent entrails. We remove the
brain, piece by piece, through the nose; we sew the eyelids shut;
we sprinkle it with ochre;

we stuff it with fruit; we stuff it with gold; we sew inside it wine and
aromatic spices, a beloved family pet—

so do we make of the emptiness of the body a vessel for the meanings we
impose upon it,

the professor told her students, who wrote all this down.

+

What would it mean to spend my last moments knowing that inside me
the surgeon's wedding ring had clotted over, grown thick and
blood-encapsulated?

His wife, anyway, had left him, his children disliked him, he'd been up all
night drinking, and left the shot glass in the body of a patient—

+

And when I opened my eyes, his face floated between mine and the
surgical lamp like God's holy visage—

+

And so I hovered high above the heads of the nurses, above the breathing
machine and its many cords, over the poles and their dangling
bags of fluid—

Death must be distinguished from dying, with which it is often
confounded, the professor said, holding up a book,

while into my body, the surgeon poured his drinks and tears, into my
body he stuffed his money, into my body he lost his children and
his wife,

into my body his distant youth vanished—

When it goes, it takes our fears with it and creates new ones, the
professor told her students, gesturing to the surgeon

who was washing his hands and crying—

+

And after a while, the professor closed her book and went home to her life.

The surgeon, too, returned to his quiet house and his fears.

My body, empty of me, lay on the table like an overstuffed bag.

Sunday Afternoon in the Park

Outside the retirement home
a dog sleeps beneath a tree.
A bus has been idling by that lamppost
for half an hour.
Some people still haven't collapsed their umbrellas,
and now the dog trots across the wet grass
toward a girl no one notices by the swing set.

Wait, I cried, but already the bus
was pulling into the street
with its load of sleeping travelers.
And far below, the girl and her dog
had vanished, too,
in the other direction.

Yes, it rained all morning,
but then the sun came out.
Someone decorated my room
with the sounds of distant traffic.
The whisper of wheels
on linoleum, then footsteps.
Pills, pills, pills, calls the crazy woman
down the hall.

How I love a cool Sunday morning
high above the park
after a rain.
If I could, I would jump
right through this window.

Immortality Lecture

There is a way to be both here and not here.

The cartoon cat stands just out of sight with the mallet.

The cartoon mouse peers from his hole into the living room.
Then yellow birds circle his head as he rises to heaven on angel's wings.

Your children have been watching TV for hours.

The cat peels the mouse from the floor,
drapes it over a piece of bread, and opens his mouth.

The sun butters the windowsill on a Saturday morning
in the summer before someone will die.

On the birthday cake, a single candle sputters like a fuse
the cat can't blow out.

The TV decorates their eyes with explosions of blue light.

Their heads are like little rooms
in which the mouse sits at his desk designing a rocket.

They will always remember you like this,
at your desk.

So the cat soars above the house and explodes.
Then the cat is in their heads designing a catapult.

I have implied that someone soon will die.

All morning, dead relatives
have marched through the room toward their rewards.

The mouse is drawing a door on the wall with chalk.
Now he is opening the door and stepping through it.

The cat has drawn a tunnel on the wall that flattens him.

Your children are bored. They've seen this one before
and are changing the channel.

You can never vanish from their world.

Two

I Am Knocking at Your Window

Cleveland, Detroit, and Lexington. Then Kansas City. Suddenly: Dallas and Houston and, on the same day, Los Angeles. Like long exhalations in a cold month—

so we moved to the mountains, then to a tunnel drilled in the mountains, and we pitched our tents there on the asphalt and ventured out some days for food and blinked in the light

(when the wind took the contagion to the south)

and when the forest burned, we gathered at the middle of the tunnel, our mouths to the floor, coughing

and those who survived buried the dead at the mouth of the tunnel then drove the mountain road toward the burned-out general store—

+

And in what cave were you hiding? Beneath what mountain? In what cool cellar, in what shopping mall, asleep in what bank vault with the pointless money, beneath what Colorado prairie where the missiles

never woke to save us, where the little wires pulse, where their hearts said *tick, tick, tick* while no one threw the switch and let them up and into the viral air?

In which hospital? In which bed?

My father, I am writing you this letter on what paper I can find: in the margins of a useless atlas of our sleeping nation.

+

Later, I woke to footsteps

and saw before me what at first I thought was you

though it was only a boy who, having wandered from his group, stumbled upon our encampment in the heart of the mountain.

One hand had withered and even in the dim light, the tell-tale tracery of scars upon his cheek—

+

Some days, we drove the empty streets and peered inside car windows where the emptied bodies of our neighbors slept.

Some days, we set them on fire and watched the smoke rise above the rooftops and at last that boy stopped crying

and, like all of us, grew fearless. Bricks to the windshields, bats to the hoods, and then a burning rag would make the gas tanks bloom

and warm our faces in the heat. And how he learned to laugh at that

as the flames calmed and at last we said we'd eat.

+

Long ago you were lying in a hospital bed

and now I am writing this letter to you. You were asleep and dreaming;

oh, my father, a book slips from your hand; the nurse takes it away.

My father, asleep as the needle drips, tipped back as she removes the tray and turns the TV off—

+

In this way, I was an imagined thing,

and am, still, an imagined thing

+

as is the boy hunting the empty streets at night, a baseball bat in his good hand and a bag in the other.

He brings to the tunnel cans of food, he brings us other people's jackets, batteries, excellent shoes, and one day, wrapped in cornhusks, a cooked fish steaming from someone else's fire.

+

(Asleep in your pajamas, asleep in your bed at home where they told you *rest, rest now,* asleep by the waterglass and the pillcup, asleep while the sun sets and the street goes quiet and in the yard the weeds grow high

and that boy and I walk the once-blasted landscape where now the moss has covered up the burned-out stumps, where now the birds returned at last, where now our town's collapsing into bent rooftops, beetles, woodsmoke.)

+

My father, I have walked to our house.

The boy recedes when I part the weeds and peer in your window. I know you're asleep,

the sunlight of a distant year sliding over the windowsills, warming your face one last morning long ago,

your breath grown thin, a circuitry of scars,

and in your head this child waiting cross-legged at the driveway's edge looking toward our tunnel in the mountain.

Show Us

Then the sun came up and all around was nothing but garbage,
the bits and gasps of broken glass, paper cups,

         newspapers calling, *Sale, Sale,*
while they tumbled down the windswept boulevards.

+

So we said to the nation, *Show us the hidden terrorists!*
but the nation was a million shoe soles,

        the nation crowded the streets
or waited at bus stops or spun in those revolving doors.

          No terrorists
and we kept walking.

    It is always business for this nation
and, for its terrorists, secrecy.

+

Show us your terrorists, we said to the ATMs

         as they flicked our money out.
Show us your terrorists, to the subway token machine,
to the newspaper box and the fireplug.
Show us,

   to the gathering clouds.

+

And when it rained, umbrellas expanded

                                  like a black mood,

beneath which the wet shoes of commerce
trod the garbage streets.

                         No terrorists.

+

Come out! Come out! We're riled about nothing without you.

We are a nation of gray old men walking rain-slick streets
beneath black umbrellas.

Fill our tall buildings with your vines and blooms, sprinkle us with glitter
and with glass,

                  with thrills and shards of foil and steel!

+

When you point the camera, we smile,

                       and the camera says *Bang!*

+

Without you,

          we go to work each day

and, on weekends, shop or sleep.

                         Come with your dark hearts

and glass tubes. Come with your metal briefcases,
perfect suits and gloves.

Oh, hollow-toothed attackers,
fleet fingered, cyber-bot, lovely and alone,
we are so nearly your bomb.

                    Come and connect our wires.

A Giant Bird

Its great heart pounded like the distant sea
wounding itself against the cliffs.

+

We lived in its shade.

Sometimes, my daughter ran her fingers along that part of the breast
that swagged low over our camp.

It's beautiful, she said, smoothing a feather's twig-like barbs,
gazing past our mountain toward the burning cities.

+

What kind of bird is it?
                                        Some feathers were tawny, others tinged a perfect white.
Is it a sparrow?
                        It may be a sparrow.
Is it an owl?
                        I can't see its face.
An eagle? I think it's an eagle.
                                        We often played this game.

+

The breezes made trails of the smoke
that rose from the distant burning cities.

Those people worshipped golden eagles.
We saw the statues winking on their plazas in the sunset.

+

Sometimes, it would soar beyond the mountains to the sea,
its black shadow slipping over the valleys.

But always it returned by evening, settling gently over us again.

+

I knew it was an eagle
from the talons curling beneath its down,

and the set of its enormous wings.

+

I'd become accustomed to the fingers of smoke
that rose on windless summer days.

What are they doing?
                    They're killing each other.
Why are they killing each other?
The bird shifted on blood-stained talons, resettled itself.
Why are they killing each other?
Their golden eagles glistened in the sun.

+

Sometimes, one city had acquired all the golden eagles.
Sometimes another city had them, or a third.
Sometimes, the golden eagles were distributed evenly among them all.

+

Those days,
            we did not worry about the rain, nor the heat of the sun,
except when the bird rose from our cliffs
and vanished in the direction of the sea
where, we knew, it ate.

+

Later,
        we learned it fed on men who fished in boats along the shore.
Later,
        it ate captured soldiers
chained to highly decorated rafts and set adrift.

+

You will have predicted by now
that one day the bird did not return.

+

All month, the cities in the valley had been quiet,
as if they'd forged a peace.

The weather, too, was sultry and unshifting.

Then up from the distant cliffs that tumbled toward the sea,
a lighter plume of smoke arose,

and when the sea winds turned, we smelled upon them burning flesh.

+

After they'd devoured it—
                    after they'd stripped the meat from its bones,
after they'd fed cubes of its heart to their dogs, after they'd
burned the plumage and hung its talons from the doorways
of their holy places—
                    they built from its bones a scaffolding,
then fastened to it feathers made of worn-out sails.

+

Its beak they built from the bound-together hulls
of two wrecked ships.

+

These days,
            there's peace in the newly gentle cities,
and freedom I had not expected.

The valley is cool when the winds rise up from the sea.

Sometimes I walk the long path from my house near the east gate,
down the ravine and up the other side,

where I come across what remains of our home.
It towers over me, its canvas ragged and whipping in the breeze,

its lashed-together bones grown white and creaking.

+

You people with your fancies and distractions
don't remember how it brooded over this valley,

how lovely it must have been, talons outstretched,
diving seawards in your afternoons.

PACIFICATION

Let the meeting of the Committee begin. Outside,
heavy-headed asters nod on delicate stems,
so who will call this meeting to order, who is present,
are we all present? Outside, planes fly low over the fields,
bellies full and opening, mosquitoes dying in the green mists
that sift from their tanks, so if we have a quorum,
let us elect a chairman, let us elect a secretary
who can take notes, can I hear a motion to elect?
The low thrum of an airplane's engine, doppler-inflected,
rising above the mists, a rumbling as the last insecticide
canisters shower the field with light— We have the report
of the subcommittee that needs our attention,
the airplanes winking in the afternoon sun, the airplanes
banking right, we have several concerns vital to the organization,
quality control, restructured delivery, obscuring mists,
will you turn away from the window, will someone please
close the blinds, those are only mosquitoes dying,
the airplanes are spraying the fields.

Orchard

Here is the orchard
where once they threw people.

The orange sleeps in its rind.
Its dreams are sour, sour,

then, months later, turn sweet
just before it falls from the branch

into rot.
Here is the place

where they lined them up
in a gentle rain

and now a cool wind blows
from a distant mountain

through the orange trees
into the past tense.

When, after surgery, your heart
stopped

the nurses ran to your bed,
hovered over you

until you smiled.
Later, they were more watchful.

Death fills us
like night will fill that old barn.

It's getting late
and raining again.

Here is the place
where they parked their trucks

to let the people out.
Here is where the soldiers

smoked during their breaks.
Now the sun has set.

Someone should have
harvested those oranges.

They are scattered around our feet.
They are falling into a pit.

CLEVELAND, OHIO

The last thing my father did was lie in bed.

A machine kept beeping. It stood by his feet and its screen glowed greenly.

The falling snow looked like insects swarming around the streetlamps.

I was afraid to turn on the light.

His hands had swollen and when he breathed the liquid in his chest grew thick so the room filled with the sound of it and no one came,

the nurses wouldn't drain his lungs, wouldn't hold his hand or cut him open, the nurses stood in the doorway and shook their heads and smiled,

said, *He's asleep, he can't feel a thing,* and increased his dose

while far away the phone rang and rang and the sky above Cleveland filled with insects

and the machine at the foot of the bed considered my father

who was sleeping and would go on sleeping forever.

+

Years later, a dog had been barking happily all evening,

and now it was past midnight and the BI-LO glowed dimly behind the apartment buildings.

Someone had chained him to a post and he greeted the passing train, the buses that rumbled down West 25th Street,

that man walking toward the intersection who stopped as if to pet him, then, under the red light, aimed carefully and shot him in the head.

The dog whimpered

long past the time when the man turned the corner and the light turned green,

and from his balcony my neighbor tilted his bottle to the evening, said, *Finally!* and went inside for the night.

+

When he inhaled, I heard a sucking sound, followed by the long rattle of his exhalation

and across the hall a woman with her back to me held a child and sang all night

and whether the intravenous tubes extended into her or into her child I could not tell

and every room was bathed by the televisions and the green light of those machines awake at the ends of the beds

until I looked out the window and into the snow where years later a man would shoot a dog at the intersection of West 25th Street and Jay Avenue.

+

The dog was still whimpering, its legs twitching, and when I reached through the fence to pat him

he tapped his tail happily against the grass and when I walked away, he whined,

so I returned. It took that dog half an hour to die.

+

He is still barking into the very same night my father sleeps in now,

having made death, at least, a thing to be slipped into quietly and recalled as breathing

that slows and rattles while the nurse says, *He is comfortable, it won't be long,* and increases his dose

and I cannot know if he is dreaming or merely emptied,

and that woman wrapped in tubes holds her child and sings

and Cleveland spreads out around us, the Terminal Tower's cold lights, the glowing green arrows up Carnegie Avenue, and the red arrows,

Shaker Heights, Beachwood Place buried in snow, the mall like a great machine blinking along the edge of the highway.

A Story About Dying

The old cat was dying in the bushes.
Its breaths came slow, slow,
                              and still
it looked out over the sweetness of the back lawn,
the swaying of tall grass in the hot wind,
the way sunlight warmed the garbage can's
sparkling lid.
                    It closed its hot eyes,
then struggled them open again.

+

In unison, the dogs explained themselves
to the passing freight train.

+

I don't know where it's gone,
her husband said without looking up from his paper

while she stood on the back porch shaking the food bowl,
calling one of its names.

+

All this the dying cat observed
from beneath the bushes, its head
sideways in the grass, its fur wet where the dog
had caught it in its teeth.

+

And now there's another train,
and the dogs are explaining themselves again.

+

The food makes that sparkling sound in the metal bowl
and the cat tries to lift its body from the grass

but it's feeling hollowed out, empty and strange
as though it's floating just above the tips of grass,
as if its paws barely touch the blades' rich points.

+

We are powerful dogs, the dogs say,
                                    but we are also good,
while the vast, mysterious trains
                                    pass them by,

+

while the cat drifts above the grass tips,
and the sun is so bright the yard sparkles,

and wouldn't it be nice to rest there
on the garbage can's hot lid, on the car's hood?

But it wants the food glittering in the metal bowl,
the food that, also, drifts above the grass tips.

+

And then the cat floats down the tracks,
the train's long call a whistling in its head

+

while the dogs explain themselves again,
we are good dogs, good dogs,
                                 as the cat grows
distant, is merely a speck,
is just a taste in the mouth
of one of the chorus.

An Angel

One morning,
a shoeless old man walked down his front steps
into the melting snow.

He couldn't remember where he'd left his car.
It wasn't under the carport,
it wasn't parked at the curb.

So he strolled down Prospect Avenue
toward the pharmacy parking lot
where he must have forgotten it,

though where the pharmacy was, he couldn't recall.
And what he meant to buy there eluded him, too,

and, anyway, he had forgotten his wallet,
and where was he going now?

His feet had been hurting him, but now they were numb,
now they felt all right, warm and strange—

And isn't it lovely how the American flag
high above the used car lot
snaps in the spring wind?

The young soldier gave him a curious look,
but didn't say anything
so the old man kept walking

because he would be late for the service,
the enormous sun beyond the steeple,
filtering orangely through wet branches,

the glare of traffic lights and onrushing cars
confusing in the darkness,

and there are only two ways this story can end,
because the old man can't walk forever
and he is unlikely to grow wings.

Love Poem

No money
and the mailbox grew wet and empty-hearted
in the rain. No money

and the ambulance's great red eye
lit someone else's
sleeping street.

They made me leave the hospital
and come home
where, moneyless, I looked out the window, into the rain.

You were empty, asleep and untouchable
in your hospital gown. Emptily,
the nurses walked past me,

their sympathetic heels chipping the linoleum.
That bruise where the IV goes
was round as the absence of a coin,

and you, asleep, the tube in your throat
both terrifying and
I don't know what to call it—

broke? Without money,
the world stops, the world's great cities
close their eyes.

Then the heart goes dead no matter how they pound it.
Without money, I keep driving
the long road from the hospital

cursing the nurses who touched my arm so gently,
said, "Go home now, there's nothing you can do."
Darling,

it's so much easier to talk about money,
to spend myself inside this poem.
Wake up.

You've slept and slept while the rain came down.
Say something, anything at all.
Open your bankrupt mouth.

Auto Wreck

Far from your damage, snow is falling.

It covers up the taxis and the buses. It covers the terminals and the
airplanes on the runways and those parked at the gates.

The old woman is saying that she has to catch her flight. She's sorry she
doesn't have identification, it's at home on the table where she left
it, she's sorry, please let me through.

And the young man shakes his head sadly and tries to explain again—

And the woman drops her plastic shopping bag at the young man's feet.
Her son is waiting for her in Cleveland, she says, he is very sick.
He's in the hospital and what can she do? Look at me, I'm an old
woman, do I look like a terrorist?

And the young man says his supervisor is on his way, that he'll sort it out—

But her plane is leaving, she says, and then she is crying because now her
plane has probably left and there she is stuck in the airport with
a storm coming on and her son in a bad way and they'll probably
cancel all the late flights now.

And the people behind her shift back and forth in line. The young man
feels their angry eyes on him.

Is there maybe someone I can call? he says. I can call someone for you. But
the woman has turned around, has walked away.

At his feet is her plastic bag.

+

One, two, three, I said, and down we went
so the snow whipped our faces raw
and when we hit the ramp, the inner-tube bounced us clear into the air.
For a moment we suspended there, your warm breath
on my cheek and both of us hollow-boned as birds.

Oh my brother, wake up.
Don't you know a thousand satellites circle the earth like gnats?
I could find our old house on this screen. I could find this hospital
          window.
I'm sorry about the snow. When they push the needle in, it buries you.

+

And the plastic bag sat on a shelf in the lost luggage room
and all night long it became thick and heavy
so the plastic stretched over what grew inside it.

So late at night, the airport was mostly empty
and in the bag his heart was slowly beating.

+

What will I do? she asks the ticket agent as the fabulous de-icers cover
          the wings with mist.
What will I do? as the plane rumbles through the snow, as it rides the
          long, low runway far from her, as it lifts gently into the air.
What will I do? as the hundred faces press against the windows and the
          plane tips dangerously, then rights itself again, rising through the
          blizzard in his skull,

up and up through the windlash and white.
My son is in the hospital, she says, watching all this through the window.

+

And some summers, we lay on the balcony and played cards with girls from
   the neighborhood.

For days, we did nothing but play cards and when it grew too hot, we
   quarreled.

+

Do not die, I was saying from the back of the line, while the old woman
   argued with the guard, while she dropped her bag at his feet and
   shouted and shook her head.

And the pained young man asked her to move aside while he radioed for help.

And we were all impatient, the line stopped dead and the snow coming down,

so when the old woman stormed off, I was relieved. The man next to me
   sighed, said she wasn't no terrorist, they should just let her through,

and, the line moving again, I agreed.

+

The truth is, my brother, you are asleep in your bed and in your head it is snowing

and I have already told you about sledding and I have asked you about the
satellites and those long summers when we played on the balcony
with the girls whose names I can't remember.

And the truth is, I am looking out the hospital window into the street,
this laptop balanced on my knees.

And the truth is, I never heard a word that old woman said, though she
looked half-crazy and, still, I think they should have let her
through.

I flew all night to get here, making up the story about that old woman

and still you can't hear me, though the doctor says it's ok to talk, how can
it hurt?

+

I can find our old house on the laptop's screen, and I can zoom in on it.
There's the balcony, seen from above, light-speckled
and strange. I do not know who lives there now.
Do you?
        There are maybe two boys
and above their heads satellites circle the earth
taking pictures which they send on down to us.

+

And the next morning, the heart stopped beating.

And when the young man slipped into the lost-luggage room, he made
sure no one saw him.

And when he opened the bag, he found not my brother's heart, he found
not my brother's body, he found not a pile of snow, ash—

(and up we flew on the inner tube and suspended there for the longest time)

he found a child's blanket, yellow and blue, and on it a name was stitched.
It was soft and, in places, tattered,

something a mother might have made to cover up her child.

Strange Lullaby

In the flu-infected city,
the schoolchildren sleep
while overhead, the lead-inflected
sky begins to weep.

Child, child, child, their mothers say,
cold cloths to their heads.
The lamps beside them cast their glares
from night tables to beds.

Disease, like a light switch, voids the city.
The children sleep or die.
The sleeping dream of dying and
the dead ones sleep awry.

THE IDEA OF THE THING AND NOT THE THING ITSELF

The baby boy had been dreaming for too long.
Oh darling, darling boy, his mother kept saying
                            in his dream
while outside the rain came down in the stormy season
and the palm fronds fluttered in the wind.
                        Oh darling boy,
it had been so long he could not move his legs,
he could not see, his head was a rattling
                        empty thing,
Oh darling boy, she told him, rocking him by the window
in his dream,
             while, for a hundred years, he slept
in a cardboard box, he lay wrapped in white linen,
secured with ribbons
               under the floorboards
where she'd hid him when he died.

+

How, years later, a young man wanted a baby of his own.

+

One hundred years of raindrops
               in the stormy seasons,
so the palm trees bent and grew
                 and sometimes broke from the earth
so their roots splayed in the next day's sun like, he thought,
a childless old man's gnarled fingers.

+

And his wife could not conceive so, *OK,*
he said, *OK, that's fine, there are other ways,*

                    and she smiled
and he made her dinner
                because what else could he do
with his hands

+

while the baby boy slept in his box
beneath the floorboards they walked across,
                  and all night long
his little dreams rose up on strings
              and filled the house
that the morning light washed clean.

+

Oh darling baby boy,
           she'd told her baby, rocking him by the window,
the fever having passed, the trembling gone, the coughing stopped,
oh darling boy,
        as she wrapped him in a curtain and tied him with twine
and even then
        she couldn't bring him to the minister, couldn't bury him—

+

(so many things he couldn't have: a car that didn't cough and die,
a house that didn't leak,

and just listen to his wife on the phone with her mother.)

+

—but kept him in his bassinet,

and covered him with ribbons
and, later, pried the floorboards up.

+

(And what would he trade for a boy of his own
a boy that looked like him?

The money
in the bank? The house and all its moldering shingles?
The *whisperwhisperwhisper* of his wife upstairs?)

+

And *such rain,*
she told her mother, *I don't know what to do, I don't,*
as the old house creaked on its timbers
and her husband looked out the window

to where a palm tree
tipped and died.

And the baby

+

dreamed of rain tapping the windows
                                    like impatient
fingernails, the stir and lap of water rising
                                    over the porch,
under the door, bleeding into the room,

+

where the young man thought about walking out the door for good this time,
right out the goddamn door into the rain,

and *Darling baby*, his mother told him
                                    a hundred years ago,
wrapping him like a gift,

and *yes, yes, yes,* she said, crying now,
holding the phone away so her mother wouldn't hear,

+

the water spreading into the bedroom,
seeping between the cracks,
                                    down to where the idea of a baby
slept in the same old box she'd placed him in long ago,
and, for all that water,
                        would not be washed away.

Not Near Enough

Nine-fingered Lord, collateral Lord, Lord of airplanes that rise from the base,

strategic Lord, angry and strange, Lord of the surgical strike, incursion Lord, lisper and wild,

Lord over whom the thrusters thrust and the throttle shifts, Lord behind whom the afterburners flare,

Lord of aircraft and strongmen, Lord of iron rails, lockers, vigor and stink,

and when the airplanes rise against the rising sun, it is your pink light that haloes them,

and when they singe their wheels on the landing strip: your thin smoke.

Imperfect Lord under whom I've prayed, half-settled and drift-eyed: here I am

at home, in the middle of a field in the middle of the country in the middle of a war

I haven't seen, and Lord, I never flew, I never fought, but watched you thrill the sky, the screen,

dear Lord of the planes that soar overhead, blacklit, each crucifix-like silhouette,

Lord of the B2's distant roar, I have idled in my pick-up, I have stood in line,

I have seen your rain turn the sidewalks slick so the stoplights shimmer in their glare, oh, Lord of Autumn, with your thick, scarred arms, reach down through the trees,

into my yard, to my truck's lit cab, and pluck me out and carry me high, Lord, carry me high.

Acknowledgments

These poems originally appeared in the following publications:
Boulevard, Cincinnati Review, Colorado Review, Crazyhorse,
Ecotone, Explosion Proof, Field, Gettysburg Review, Indiana Review,
The Kenyon Review, lo-ball, Mixer, nor: the new ohio review,
Notre Dame Review, The Paris Review, Plume, The Southern Review,
and *The Virginia Quarterly Review.*

The poem "Strange Lullaby" borrows a line from Auden's "The Fall of
Rome."

These poems were written with the support of a fellowship from the
Lannan Foundation.

Enormous thanks to Sally Ball, Hadara Bar-Nadav, Noah Blaustein,
Martha Collins, Mary Hallab, Joy Katz, & Wayne Miller, who offered
close readings and advice about these poems. And to Martha Rhodes
for her generosity and support.

This book is dedicated to Wayne Miller, friend and collaborator.

Kevin Prufer is the author of five previous collections, including *In a Beautiful Country* (a finalist for the Rilke Prize and the Poets' Prize) and *National Anthem* (named one of the five best poetry books of the year by *Publishers Weekly*), both from Four Way Books. He also co-curates the Unsung Masters Series and has edited several anthologies, including *New European Poets* (Graywolf, 2008; w/ Wayne Miller) and *New Young American Poets* (Southern Illinois UP, 2000). The recipient of three Pushcart prizes, multiple *Best American Poetry* selections, and fellowships from the NEA and the Lannan Foundation, he teaches in the creative writing program at the University of Houston and the Lesley University Low Residency MFA program.